INVISIBLE SEA

KEVIN BUSHELL

INVISIBLE SEA

Cover illustration by Alain Reno.
Author photograph by Marilyn Gillespie.
Book designed and typeset by Primeau Barey, Montreal.
Edited by Keith Henderson.

Legal Deposit, Bibliothèque et Archives nationales du Québec
and Library and Archives Canada, 1st trimester, 2022.

Library and Archives Canada Cataloguing in Publication
Title: Invisible sea / Kevin Bushell.
Names: Bushell, Kevin, author.
Description: Poems.
Identifiers: Canadiana 2022015855X | ISBN 9781927599570 (softcover)
Classification: LCC PS8603.U8253 I58 2022 | DDC C811/.6–DC23

For our publishing activities, DC Books gratefully acknowledges the financial
support of SODEC and of the Government of Canada through Canadian Heritage
and the Canada Book Fund. *Nous reconnaissons l'aide financière du gouvernement
du Canada.*

**Société
de développement
des entreprises
culturelles**
Québec ❦❦ Canadä

Printed and bound in Canada.
Interior pages printed on Enviro Book, an environmentally responsible paper
containing 100% post-consumer recycled fiber, processed chlorine-free and
manufactured using biogas energy.
Distributed by LitDistCo.

DC Books
5 Fenwick Avenue
Montreal West, Quebec H4X 1P3
www.dcbooks.ca

Contents

*The airplane has replaced the bird in the imagination
as the symbol of the release of spirit from the bonds of earth.*

–Joseph Campbell

*So then to unimagined arts
He set his mind and altered nature's laws.*

–Ovid, *Metamorphoses,* Daedalus and Icarus

TOOL AND DIE

Before airplanes, before bicycles, you built words,
blackened fingertips arranging letters like beads
on a string, upside-down and backwards. Before

words it was a press made of carriage parts
and an old tombstone, rising and falling to the roar
of engine, whir of paper through rollers,

one thousand sheets per hour. And before
the press, you built the letters themselves,
one by one, carved into woodblocks.

I see you as a boy, the cube pinned
against your chest while your mouth forms
in tandem the phonemes your pocketknife

scribes, uttering, as if for the first time,
the alphabet, that first tool we use
to build our words, our worlds.

KILL DEVIL HILL

THE DEATH OF OTTO LILIENTHAL

Sacrifices must be made.
(final words of O. L.)

2000 flights. 2001 a botch,
the legs swung forward
in a sort of two-footed *whoops!*
as the glider pitches into a stall,
comes to rest in that breathless
moment of the fall when one is
suspended in perfect knowledge: Oh shit!
before gravity does its stuff.

But this is no slip on your ass. This
is fifty feet of helpless, backwards terror:
a car stuck in reverse, floored, no brakes,
and a brick wall behind you
the size of a mountain.
You know nothing of ailerons, only
the shifting of weight, the centre of gravity, forces
that now, finally, defeat you.

*

This news comes to me
in the form of a newspaper clipping
held in the hand at Orville's bedside, a heavy
persistent *Why?* pulling at the margins.

I turn it over and over
as Orville spins in and out of waking,

dreaming in typhoid delirium
of windmills, propellers, the hands of clocks and drafting
    compass
forming perfect circles.

Six weeks later the fever will break.
He'll sit up in bed eating tapioca—a near death.

But in that other death
a burning issue is born.

GROUNDED

Before I could fly I
had to get dinged in the head with a hockey stick,
knocking me to the ice. No big deal,

I think, and skate it off. But when, two weeks later,
my heart begins to precipitate flight, fluttering
like a caged bird, I know

my college days are done.
Friends leave home, launch careers, start families,
while my future collapses to the size of a house.

Six months moping through its empty rooms and I
discover a gravity with doubt at its core,
a sort of black hole tugging throughout the night.

I decide to launch myself headlong
into the role of cook and chambermaid to my dying mom,
becoming the butt of Orville's jokes, three full years

reading at her bedside for the education
I missed at Yale, and something more,
watching her own slow descent.

WING-WARPING

To learn how it's done
I watch the birds, those old hats,
how they twist one wingtip up and
one down in a how-do-you-do wave
good-bye, turning their backs on us
because they can.

I spend months in the study
searching through Pettigrew's *Animal Locomotion*
and Marey's *Animal Mechanism,* their white,
   many-feathered wings
spread wide across my desk. When I've had enough I
hop on my bike and

go like hell, bent low over the handlebars,
banking hard through turns
to feel the pull of all three planes
in one sweeping arc.

But it's here in the shop where, oddly enough,
I find my answer, idly playing
with an empty inner-tube box, thinking outside
it might be a biplane held in both hands, how
one corner goes up when
one goes down, a simple twist
to unlock the secret of human flight.

$$L = k \times S \times V^2 \times C_L$$

Lift in pounds equals
the fingertips of air, all fifty million
pall-bearers who will give the old heave-ho
to my useless body, plus the machine,
onto the shoulders of wind—and off

this damned earth, thumbing my nose at gravity,
who can only shrug, knowing he's been outwitted
for now. Then

I'll rise, as if cross-legged on a carpet, hover
in a headwind squared, times my faith,
but not in God, Silly—in Smeaton's and Lilienthal's tables,
coefficients that neatly plug into my plans, leaving me
only the maths
to calculate the wingspan of my desire.

CROSSING THE ALBEMARLE SOUND

The first lesson in Applied Aerodynamics
takes place not on the glider
but aboard Israel Perry's schooner.

Nightfall as we head off
out of the mouth of the Pasquotank
into the sound, Israel uneasy as the sea

leaps into the gathering breeze,
suddenly shifts to south-east,
and builds to gale.

The large cabin strikes the headwind flush
and soon we are soaring—static
in the onrushing air, the sea

pounding the hull from below.
A gust tears the foresail from the boom
with a roar, but I gather it back

as the boat pitches and rolls in the dark,
drifting closer to the rocky shoulder
of the lurking shore.

Israel decides to round the point
but before we can reach the light
another gust rips the mainsail free,

and now there is nothing else to do
but run the sandbar
with nothing but a jig, pray

the flat bottom will clear
as waves break high over the stern
and swamp the deck.

I don't know how Israel is able
to turn in such a sea without capsizing, but he does,
and we find shelter in the channel for the night.

I collapse on deck exhausted,
drenched by the sea and dream
not of flight but falling, tumbling

down toward a darkness
black as night but without sky,
without air.

LADIES NIGHT AT THE WESTERN SOCIETY
OF ENGINEERS, 1901

Our failed experiments
have us down in the dumps,
so I decide to retrace our steps—not backwards
but from the top, a slow-motion replay
of the descent and crash of our career.

It's Chanute's idea
and I fall for it, suckered in
with a little nagging from sis. They know
what I need now most
is a kick in the butt, and what better boot
than one from a society of engineers?

I spend weeks preparing the speech and lantern slides,
determined at least to leave an accurate record.
Asked if it will be witty or scientific,
I answer pathetic, a sign
that Old Man Gravity
has me in his grip again.

But it works. Seventy members and their wives
have come to hear my analysis.
Katherine says I never looked so swell
dressed in Orville's suit and cuffs,
and when I call for the lights to be dimmed,
there I am, backlit by the sun,
set against the sky and soaring
clear over the heads
of ladies and gentlemen.

$L = k \times S \times V^2 \times C_L$ (revised)

Not within fifty years will man fly.
–Wilbur Wright, 1901

Lift in pounds equals
one-third our projections, dammit,
the maths adding up to one
bum steer in trusting those tables, off by enough
to make the machine a flop.

We become skeptics, start again
from scratch, whipping up a wind tunnel
from an old packing crate, a window cut in one side
to see for ourselves the bulging bicep of air.

Other men had tried and failed,
and we do too until we build a translator
of hacksaw blades and bicycle-wheel spokes
and learn language of air.

By mid-December we feel
we might soon be able to speak
back to the wind, but it will take
another two full years to construct our answer.

FIRST FLIGHT: COMPOSED ON THE CENTENNIAL OF THE BIRTH OF FLIGHT

Five weeks hanging about camp, pulling stumps
for firewood, waiting for parts, waiting
for new parts when those break, waiting
for the weather, then finally—
to hell with it let's try, head-on
into a suicidal headwind.

The lifeguards are signaled, trudge
across the sand to serve as witnesses,
cheering party, the world's first ground crew,
muscle the machine into position
on the runway rail. The props are pulled—
and the engine coughs to life.

While it's warming, the two of you
withdraw from the group, holding hands
like two friends parting.

Orville climbs onto the wing and
slips the lever to set the machine
inching down the track, so slowly
you only have to trot alongside
to steady the wing, forty feet
when the machine, almost unexpectedly
rises from the rail.

In the famous photograph, you stand
framed on the right, frozen awkwardly
like an action figure, apparently alarmed.
In posterity Orville gets the credit
yet our eyes land on you, solitary figure
in a landscape barren as the moon,
dressed head to toe in black
as if in mourning, but it would be
about a hundred years before we'd know
what had died, who you killed.

THE OUTER BANKS

Everywhere we go we are called Mr. Wright
and need no introduction. We appeared one day

on the Bankers' shores dressed head-to-toe in black
like Mad Mabe, the witch of Nags Head Wood,

but the locals don't pay tribute to us.
These God-fearing people are wary

of our experiments up on Kill Devil Hill
and our Yankee ways. Orv and I

have ruined the local economy,
buying up all the eggs and

hoarding them up in the hills. At night,
the bobbing light of our lantern looks like

one swung by wreckers in another century
to lure ships onto the shoals

where the cargo could be stolen.
Or Blackbeard's. This is a place of legends,

and we, the Bishop's boys, have come here
to become one. On a cold December day

we climb aboard our white-winged bird,
slip the surly bonds of earth,

and send a boy running through the streets
screaming, "Damned if they ain't flew!"

THE CANARD

An early eyewitness account of the flying machine

Imagine, my friends, a duck
whose nodding head out front
is an elevator with a biplane bill.
It looked just like that.

       Now imagine
its wings—great white twenty-foot wings
like . . . like a streetcar with the sides knocked out, or
or a locomotive, an aluminum locomotive,
without wheels
that's left its track
sideways
and is steaming straight at you.

It looked just like that.

Its heart is a waste-paper basket
glowing red and driving in circles
two large flapping tail-feathers. I tell you

it is indescribable, this flying machine,
with its operator lying prostrate inside
like a minnow swallowed whole, feet first.

FLIERS OR LIARS

Three years to solve the ageless problem,
five to sell the solution on good faith and our word.
No one wants it. They want instead
"the moment of miracle"—when the wheels kiss the earth
good-bye before they'll
put their money down.
But we're nobody's fools. Orv and I
keep the machine locked in the hangar
and the photos close to our chests.

The French call us *bluffeurs* and
struggle into the air in wicker baskets.
When the chance finally comes we
prove it, flying figure eights
that send witnesses walking off the field
muttering "My God, my God…"

HOMECOMING

After all my calculations, I never predicted this.
Any hope of a quiet family reunion
is dashed at the station. As the train pulls in,
I see the streets black with people.
Flags, banners, balloons flap and flail
from lampposts. The train-whistle blows
to announce my arrival, and the factories of Dayton
echo in the distance. Somewhere
a band is playing "Home, Sweet Home."

I've been away for over a year
in France, Italy, Germany, followed closely
by thousands who flock to see me fly.
I can't even take a bath without the curious
peeking between slats of the hangar!

Princes and millionaires are thick as thieves
I once wrote Orville, but I prefer
to eat my lunch with the local workmen.
I like the way they mangle my name, *Vieille Burette,*
turning me into an old oilcan, and how
their callused hands gesticulate gracefully
over their plates like soiled birds. It is my only relief
from the relentless crowds, except when I disappear
on my bicycle into the forest
where even the press dare not follow.

Now all I want is home cooking and familial conversation.
The train trembles to a halt
and ten thousand people lurch forward to greet me.
The Home Guard is overwhelmed
and soon the platform fills with Daytoners

welcoming home their son.
Some even climb the carriage walls,
and when their arms begin to plunge
through the partially open windows I
shrink back into the cushions, horrified
by hands blindly reaching, grasping,
searching for something solid,
finding only air.

LE PAPIER BLEU

8:00 a.m. and I am preparing for a try
at the *Coupe Michelin* when the news arrives
on the ominous blue paper of a French cablegram.
CRASH AT FORT MYER SELFRIDGE KILLED
  ORVILLE INJURED
STOP. I retire to the hangar for privacy.

Some say I broke down weeping, the same steady hand
that had piloted the trials of the day before
now shaking like an aspen. Some say
I paced feverishly about The Flyer,
bending a piece of wire absentmindedly
as if trying to solve some mechanical problem.
Some say I dropped to my knees and prayed.

Truth is I receive this information
the same as wind speed, direction, drift,
had calculated for it as the unknown variable—
an unexpected gust, a broken prop, a lapse of judgment.
I remove the paper from my shirt pocket
and study it again, the words
an equation I have to solve.

When I re-emerge I announce
no more flights for a week, then climb onto my bike
and make for Le Mans, and those
who had gathered that day to see me fly
watch me cycle off instead
beneath a blank sheet of blue sky
not knowing what word I would find there.

FINAL FLIGHT

Orville says I look like death warmed over,
white as a ghost each time I return from the lawyers.
The last six years have been spent in court
instead of the air. No wonder we kept our secrets
so guarded. We knew this would happen,
the thieves who bribe the army guard and
slip into the hangar to steal our knowledge, a theft
even our airtight patent couldn't prevent.
They know the ropes, the legal loopholes.

In my final letter, I give our lawyer shit
for letting the case drag on so long
and our fortune slip away, but it
isn't about the money. Never has been.
I want to use those loopholes to hang
every thief and lying scoundrel from the trees,
purge the earth before taking to the sky, to be
what I've always been, the Bishop's boy.

Some say I was killed by bad shellfish in Boston.
Orville meets me at the dock, but I am not myself.
After the family picnic, I complain of a temperature
and the doctor is called, then another.
The fever worsens, and when my bladder begins to fail
I send for a secretary and witness.
That night Father sleeps with his clothes on.

The official cause is typhoid fever.
In fact, in the ways of the world,
I was burned.

BIRDMEN

THE CRAFTSMAN

Each dawn the old man climbed the palace steps
to the roof, a fishing net draped over his shoulders.
Repetition had perfected his technique. Three loud claps
then he'd hurl the net as if into the sea,
watch it unfurl in the air before sinking out of sight.

By the time the boy roused from sleep the courtyard
was littered with pink and bloodied carcasses, embryonic
and stinking in the early heat. Sometimes
he'd watch the old man lift one to the sun
and extend its wings to study the structure beneath.

Construction continued behind a locked door
well into the night, melting wax in thimbles and pinning
    each feather
precisely on plans laid out across the bedroom floor.
By spring one set was completed. The second, done quicker,
was ready mid-summer. Only then did he reveal to the boy
    his scheme.

The next morning the two this time climb the steps,
the boy frightened, the old man concerned. They help
    each other
with the elaborate straps that fasten enormous wings
to arms and back, then like courting doves
groom each other's feathers. The sun climbs out of the sea

before them and the palace stirs. They must go,
but first the old man turns to face the boy, their
    wings collide
in an awkward embrace. "Fly neither too high

nor too low," he instructs, and the boy,
as they so often do, replies "I know."

At first the boy stays close lest something go awry,
and the two fly in tandem. But soon the power he gained
intoxicates and he climbs higher. Such power in the
    slightest thing,
he thinks, a feather, unaware that the real power
is of his father's mind. The old man pleads,

bribes, commands the boy but cannot bring him back,
sees him now set overhead against the midday sun
and feels hot wax drip upon his back.
Feathers shed, the wings shred, and the boy,
now panicked, plummets past, flailing in vain

first the air, then the sea. The old man can only circle
and listen to the cries, watch in horror and curse
as the boy sinks further still beneath the waves,
leaving the craftsman bereft above a black expanse
speckled with white feathers, all that remains of his
    best creation.

THE SHORT, HAPPY FLIGHT OF KING BLADUD

He was clever, no doubt.
He tamed the underground thermal sea
at Bath, so it was only natural
to try the ethereal sea above.

Three long years he toiled,
ignoring the whispers of his subjects,
the advice of counsel and Queen,
even the gods.

He modeled wings after magpies
that so often thieved him, their nests
woven from twigs and gold necklaces
and set with mud high in the castle walls.

His wings were the same
black and white of birch bark, sewn
in layers like feathers, braced
by willow wands and held fast

with mud harvested
from the castle moat. He applied
the same persistence to this necromancy
as he did in war, and won.

When his aides saw him rise
into the air they dropped
to their knees and prayed,
not in thanks, but for mercy.

It was in vain. When the gods
brought him down upon the Temple of Apollo,

dashing him to countless pieces,
their message was clear enough.

THE FLYING MONK

Thou art come! A matter of lamentation to many
a mother art thou come;
I have seen thee long since; but I now behold thee
much more terrible,
threatening to hurl destruction on this country.

–Brother Eilmer of Malmesbury upon
seeing Halley's Comet, 1066

He looks pretty silly in his bird costume, perched
on the abbey tower, a real public spectacle
better than circus sideshow. With unorthodox wings
strapped to arms and legs, he climbs awkwardly
onto the parapet, steadies himself in the gusting Wiltshire wind.

A hundred and fifty feet below, a crowd
sways and cheers. They want to see a death.
But to him up here it sounds like jeers. Even the jackdaws
mock him with their endless circling, curious
yet wary of this other winged thing.

He's thought about this for years, the minutiae
of every moment that now, as he utters a final prayer,
it's almost familiar, like déjà vu or remembered dream, as if
this were not him—his body, his death.
How else could he do it?

Arms outstretched, he inches forward, feeling the wind,
then folds one wing over to cross himself,
a gesture mistaken below for a wave.
But his eyes are fixed on the horizon
as he waits for the wind to steady. Then leaps.

The crowd gasps and bolts as he plummets toward them,

an enormous bird of prey with wings pinned wide
    and back.
His eyes tear, nostrils flare, his mouth opens
but he chokes on his own cry, fifty feet
straight down the abbey wall he drops

before leveling off in the downward arc
of the high trapeze, clears the wall, then a tree,
    then another–
heading for the river, six hundred feet
before speed and lift and nerve leave him
stalled twenty feet up, flapping like an overgrown fledgling.

He hits the embankment to the sound of snapping ash
    and bone,
but lives to tell how he should have had a tail.
He'll hobble lame through the abbey's hallways
well into his eighties and be the first to see
the ominous tail of Halley's Comet arc through
    the heavens.

JACOB DEGEN, THE SWISS FLAPPING FLIER

Time flies, but not in his dingy shop. Most afternoons,
amid a crowd of clock-faces, the minutes ground to a halt.
With magnifying monocle clenched in one eye,
he'd peer into the microcosmic world of spinning gears,
metal teeth, the hair-like curl of a central spring,
seldom rising to the steady stream of Viennese
passing before his picture window.

Some say it was this interest in mechanics
that inspired his machine, but it was,
in fact, the fluttering hemline of a lady's dress
during one such pause that led to his eureka.
He would fashion two wings in the form of parachutes,
and by applying the fabric loosely, capture and release air
in the undulating movement of jellyfish.

No one expected him to fly, least of all him.
90 lbs. of upward force is less than half that needed,
but suspended beneath a hydrogen balloon he made
large, slow-motion, lunar leaps through the teeming
    crowds—
not exactly flight, but something suggesting it. No wonder
the public was so gullible. A few enterprising journalists
failed to mention the balloon, and he and his act

grew into myth, a modern Icarus, flew
as far as England. But it was not to last. The truth
caught up to him one windy day in Paris
when he and balloon were dragged about the field
all afternoon while the crowd grew restless,
turned ugly, gathered a force of its own,
and descended on him in a swarm of swirling arms.

THE FLIGHT OF THE SYCAMORE SEED

The one way that presents itself is to copy nature.
–Sir George Cayley

The man who discovered flight
found it one afternoon, dropped
from a tree like Newton's apple
with a wing, an idea that landed
in whirling arm experiments.

The apparatus was simple: a balance
with a plane of fabric angled at one end.
For constant force, he harnessed gravity
using a weighted string wound
round a central spindle
      and dropped
down the main staircase at High Hall, high enough
to calculate the coefficient of air.

Archimedes knew of air resistance; but Cayley saw
in a seed the lifting force of flight
and applied it to design
and name the first human copy.

X, y, z

Sir George Cayley invents the airplane (1804)

It should have been a no-brainer
to divide flight in three,

but maybe because our feet
are fixed to the earth we

could only imagine it as up. If only
we could lift, our myths explained,

flight as levitation—a kind of
drifting upwards

then carried on the winds.
Maybe that's where he was

when he doodled in his schoolbook
the weathervane of forces acting on a wing

and solved—in a leap
the ancient problem. Another sketch

would include wing, stabilizer, rudder—
a plane for each plane, the airplane,

the tool we use today
to take us anywhere.

PARIS, LE 22 OCTOBRE 1880

Mon cher et distingué monsieur Giffard:

I am entrusting to you these drawings. It seems fitting you should receive them, as you were my last hope in completing this project. For years I have gone around Paris with my hand out like a pauper, but have received nothing but criticism and personal insult. I have come to the conclusion that the gentlemen of the *Société* will only support their own theories. They are not interested in flight, only in being the first to fly, and have done everything to obstruct my progress.

I turned to you—a man of vision and passion. But the manner in which you received me the other day indicates that you agree with the *Société* as to the value of my latest design. I therefore feel that my life and work are complete. I can offer no more to French aeronautics than I have, and it has been rejected.

When I took up my studies, I thought the challenges and obstacles to flight resided in the air, but they are of the earth, between men, and within one's capacity to be free of personal ambition and petty jealousies. Until that is the case, we shall never be free, either on earth or in the air.

You must not hold yourself to blame for what I am about to do. It is my own failing in not possessing the ability to convince you and others of my ideas. I fear my life is a complete failure, amounting to nothing more than a few toys for children. My ideas and dreams shall die with me, so I am presenting you my drawings in this way, prepared for a fitting burial. I only ask that you do not place them with me after I am gone, for they have already caused me too much pain. I had wished to see the fulfillment of my dreams. Now I see I erred to dream at all.

Finally I shall be free of the earth and this body. My hip is causing me unbearable pain these days, more than you or anyone can imagine, but not more than is in my heart.

Adieu,
Alphonse Pénaud

THE LIFE OF ALBERTO SANTOS-DUMONT:
A TRAGEDY IN TWO ACTS

Who says elephants can't fly?
His did, all over Paris, a regular sight
tethered patiently over the Champs-Elysées
while he took his morning coffee, and above the Bois
    de Boulogne
as he paused for an afternoon aperitif.

His life story could rival a Hollywood movie, especially
    the part
where he walks out onto the keel of his airship
without safety lines or parachute, makes the repairs, and wins
the Archdeacon's Prize in a real nail-biter.
He even splits the award between his mechanics
and the city's beggars. Great stuff!

It could also be a Jules Verne novel
like he read in his boyhood Brazil, a fast-paced plot
filled with close calls, like when he beat out the onboard fire
with his straw hat, or was rescued from a window ledge
of the Hôtel Trocadéro, or when he crashed
into the Rothschild estate, only to be greeted by the butler
serving drinks and snacks.

It could almost be a comedy—the dapper, quirky,
    superstitious little man
makes big in Paris, wooed into the highest social circles—
except for the ending. The man with the agility of a cat
develops multiple sclerosis, retires from flying,
turns melancholic, and burns all his papers,

blaming himself for air warfare. At his homecoming,
a plane filled with dignitaries makes a pass
and bites it in the harbour. He calls off the celebrations
to search in vain himself.

In the final scene, civil war breaks out.
He learns of Brazilian bombing Brazilian,
and the happy-go-lucky guy
is found tethered by the neck, a death
so shocking it makes peace.

FOR THE RECORD

Augustus Moore Herring confesses from the grave

I can't believe how easy it was
to lie. That glide of 359 feet
I said I made in Michigan was more
like 200, but Chanute believed me.
As long as it was possible. And back then,
who knew what was possible?

That was the beginning. My claim
ballooned to over 900 feet, and soon
mendacity became for me like drink
or the drugs that were to keep me steady.
I said I created the first gasoline engine.
I said I flew before the Wrights.
I said I had a plane
that could be transported in a suitcase, and fell

in over my head. My fainting
at Kitty Hawk was feigned
to get me out of testing Chanute's contraption
when I lost my nerve, but the breakdowns
were real, and the nervous prostration.
I didn't start the fire that destroyed my warehouse
but was happy it happened.
My life had become chimerical
and needed to be razed.

So, here is my confession:
I never meant to lie.
I never meant to harm or steal.
I wanted only to fly

but found, in the end, that I
could not except in mind

and it drove me crazy.
One night in camp at Kitty Hawk I cried
out that the chicken had been stolen by a fox.
Orville wrote that it was all a joke
but the truth is it was a dream, a vision
in which I was the fox
and flight was the chicken.

CROSSING LA MANCHE

Louis Blériot flies the Dover Straits, 1909

9 years, 10 planes, 50 accidents, 750,000 francs
to learn the trick of crashing, a leap of faith
from cockpit onto the wing
at the last possible moment, breaking the fall
as well as the wing. Each time the crowd rushes forward
expecting to find him dead, instead
sees him climb from the wreckage, bewildered and annoyed.

Now broke, he tries his luck one last time,
gambling his wife's inheritance
in a race across England's old defence
from Calais to Dover, a last ditch
attempt to save his company with the £1000 prize.
His rival is set up in Sangatte, but the real opponent
is the weather—rain, fog, and wind
leave him grounded for weeks, scrutinizing the sky.

*

2:30 a.m. and he is roused from sleep
with report of a break in the weather,
is helped into coveralls and a cork vest,
his throbbing foot a stinging reminder of the last fiery mishap,
then hobbles to the dining room for coffee with his wife.
There is no time for breakfast.

At the shoreline, a small crowd has gathered to see him off.
He climbs into the cockpit, ties his crutches onto the plane,
then stands to address the crowd: "If I cannot walk,
I will show the world I can fly!" The prop is pulled

and the Anzani engine coughs and fires to life, killing a dog
that runs into the propeller.

Only now does this bad omen give him pause.
He sits quietly in the cockpit, gazing out over the Channel
while five burly men hold back the straining plane.
The sun crests behind him, catches whitecaps
ahead to the horizon as he asks himself,
Will I finish? Can I reach Dover?
This time there can be no crash.

*

None of this he remembers
long after the accolades,
not when he nearly clipped
telegraph wires on takeoff,

not when the engine, overheating,
coughed and stuttered, slowed,
and the wing dropped toward
the leaping waves, not even

when luck saved him once again
with an unexpected shower
that cooled the steaming engine
so he did not ditch,

but that moment of perfect stillness,
no ship, person, landmark in sight, suspended
in fog as if motionless, aimless, lost—
just before the first glimpse of shore.

RUCHONNET'S CIGAR

Sometimes a cigar is just
a plane, but a very fast one,
a bullet with wings, a bomb
that plunges into the earth
one test flight, leaving
a young wife destitute.

It's a start. The next day,
someone who snitched the idea
flies faster than anyone's gone before—
over 90 miles per hour!

It seems that to be light *and* strong,
one only needs to think of the sea
pounding the ship's hull, and then

let the fuselage be a boat
made of many-layered strips of wood,
a wall of leaves, a book, two
papier-mâché or birch bark canoes
joined at the gunwales. Got it?

Simple. Sleek. Strong. Beautiful.
The Monocoque. The Cigar. The plane
at the 1912 Gordon Bennett race
that blows the competition away.

DEAR SAINT-EX: THE AUTHOR ADDRESSES
THE LITTLE PRINCE

I didn't much like your parable, thought you should
get over yourself and dump the red rose.

She sounds like a bitch, a real Princess,
and what you need most is a mother.

And what do you have against businessmen, anyway?
Is it their love of money, your having had

to beg it all those years from Mom?
I read about you in Jung, *puer eternus,* momma's boy,

flying boy. Oh you were brave—you played the part
of the *enfant terrible* exquisitely, the courage

you found in the air akin
to the calculated recklessness of youth.

It must have been heaven
on your Saharan asteroid, far

from anything adult except the mail,
equally precious, especially yours

with its flights of fancy and
condescending tone. When you crashed

in the desert, went missing for days, I bet
you loved how the world waited

for some sign of your return.
You disliked Geography, but I think

it was really the earth you hated,
preferring the clean, unpopulated skies,

the sand, the stars. You are in your element now,
wherever you are, disappeared

into thin air, the only way you could go,
the final arc and crash of your airplane

a perfect question mark.

THE SPIRIT OF SAINT LOUIS

lives on in an airplane
that connects His country

to the New World in 33½ hours
flat, a feat not even a king could imagine.

It would take a farm-boy
lying in blowing wheat to wonder

what such a flight would look like
and design a plane around it.

He would have to fly blind, a gas tank
where the windshield would be,

and navigate postal-service style
with a map laid out across his lap

and the constellations spread above.
He'd place his faith

in a single engine, as we all do, the heart's
humble work a model for the millions

of perfect explosions needed
to get him there. Everything else

was shed—radio, lights, gas gauge—
a bare-bones approach that, mid-Atlantic,

left even his body behind
when the fuselage filled with spirit.

DEAR GEORGE: THE LOST LETTER

I'll admit my big break came
from my looks. You said
when I walked into your office, you knew
you'd found your woman. Lucky,
I guess, how much I looked like Lindy,
although I never liked the nickname.
No woman likes to be compared
to a man. They said I even
moved like him, shared the same
DNA and fear of fame. I can't complain,

but it wasn't easy climbing into that plane
with a drunk, putting my life in his
trembling hands. I saw the bottle
tucked behind his seat and would have
thrown it out the hatch but knew
from Daddy how that ends. Instead,
I helped carry him to the dock, managed
our "personnel problem" as best I could.
They didn't let me fly, just the easy
bit over land, and that's why

when I did it myself, solo, it was
like a single finger held up to the world
as if to say, "Women can do this too."
Nobody thought I could, even you.
And more. Records fell like tickertape,
didn't they—altitude, distance, time
merely obstacles of the mind, my body
just another obstacle, an accident of sex,

not tomboy but woman who
only wants what's fair and true.

Don't patronize me! I said I wouldn't
fly the derby if the girls and I
started east, the guys getting the harder route
over the mountains, and meant it. When
they kicked us out of the Bendix Trophy
I'd had enough; they could find another
to fly their starlet to the race. Even in marriage
I only ever asked for freedom. The note
I wrote on our wedding day said I'd never claim
anything from you and asked the same.

So, dear, if you're reading this you know
I did not make it home. Maybe it's for
the best; I was only ever afraid
of growing old, as most women will attest,
and preferred to go in my plane.
And since we've always been this honest,
there is one thing more: the rumours
that I was pregnant when I flew
round the earth's belly are true, but
the baby wasn't yours. I think you knew.

Love,
A.E.

THE WALL

Chuck Yeager breaks the speed of sound

If the sky is a sea, this is the shore, cliffs
against which we crash, becoming spray.
He wants to be history, the first to hit
the limit of air, the speed of sound
test pilots have named with metaphor.

But a wall is meant to be climbed, and this one
he will scale with six hundred gallons
of liquid oxygen, four rocket chambers, one
trim switch rigged to the stabilizer
that tips it one or two degrees, just enough
to nose the aircraft over.

He approaches in steps
.02 Mach in size, feeling his way
in the air, crunching the data
on the ground. When he
loses control of pitch, the plane
locked in level flight, it
doesn't take a scientist to tell him
he's there.

All he needs now is courage,
that quality which is really only faith
in himself, in science, in every single thing
that has brought him here, before the wall
with a fist fast enough
to punch right through.

GODSPEED

John Glenn orbits Earth

None of his missions in WWII
nor those in Korea would be like this. For one
the enemy isn't human, if there is an enemy at all.
This is merely flexing muscle, some stretching,
three laps around the earth as warm-up
for the marathon to the moon and back.

But first he must get off the ground.
The force of the earth's attraction on his body
is more than he ever felt pulling hard
through turns over the Yalu, yet nothing
compared to the pressure in outer space
of the whole world watching, a giant blue eyeball
staring straight at him.

But he doesn't screw up (his worst fear,
worse than death). The centrifuge and simulator
have prepared him well, and everything goes to plan.
The capsule pivots on command
and now he's hurtling backwards, away from the sun
which drops behind the Pacific
as lights flicker on like stars across Australia.

Three times he sees the sun set
and rise, three times the mysterious sparkling snowflakes
swirl past his window, three days
to everyone else's one, so that
when he returns to us, half pushed,
half pulled, he's forever out of sync with his kind,
never quite at home again
having travelled through both space and time.

INVISIBLE SEA

Real singing is a different kind of breath.
A nothing-breath. A ripple in the god. A wind.

–Rainer Maria Rilke, *Sonnets To Orpheus*

THE CONTINUITY EQUATION, LATE 15th C.

AV = constant

*The volume of water passing at any given point
in the river is constant.*

Slow rivers run deep, da Vinci observed,
not giving a damn for metaphor
or personality type, only
how the hell to fly—the conquest of air.

It doesn't take a genius
to notice this, but it does to see
that rivers relate to flight
as water resembles air, as
fluid

flowing

constantly.

THE VELOCITY-SQUARED RULE, 1673

$$L = \frac{1}{2}\rho V^2 SC_L \ \& \ D = \frac{1}{2}\rho V^2 SC_D$$

Lift is not directly related to velocity but velocity squared.

Lift and drag, the bipolar personality of air, relate
not to speed, but speed squared, speed
on speed, twin speed junkies.
Double the dose and you end up
in orbit, so high the hangover
is splashdown.

The aerodynamic two-step—one foot forward,
one foot back, or maybe
both feet forward—or none, lifting
clean off the dance-floor
into the air, which is all hands
with more clutch and grab
than a rugby scrum, making you
earn every inch.

So if you wanna go to heaven
don't just stand there! Get up a head of speed
and be a blade cutting through the crowd, undetected.
Ghostlike. Godlike.
Gone.

THE BERNOULLI PRINCIPLE, 1734

$$p_1 + \frac{1}{2}\rho V_1^{\,2} = p_2 + \frac{1}{2}\rho V_2^{\,2}$$

In a flowing fluid, as the velocity increases,
the pressure decreases, that is,

there's no sightseeing on the Autobahn
or window shopping when running errands.

The faster you go, the less tempted you are
to be diverted, distracted, even to glance sideways.

Sprinters stare straight ahead, focused on the finish,
after which they wave to the crowd

as momentum unwinds through the first turn.
But what if, say, you *want* to be diverted,

not to the side but up, need
a little lift, a pick-me-up?

Then you must make yourself an airfoil
whose upper surface is a fast-talking salesman.

Be a sucker, if only for a moment, pulled in
by the "less-is-more" line, duped

into sending it all to the Sally Ann
as you drift away, absent-mindedly

en route, off course.

THE EULER EQUATIONS, 1753

Aeronautics comes of age.

I. The Continuity Equation (revised)

$$\frac{\partial \rho}{\partial t} + \nabla \cdot (\rho V) = 0$$

Old Man River is really
now and now and now
but diced to smithereens,
so small and fast it's
an animated movie
with particles as pictures

grown too big for their britches,
bulging and pressing their way
into presence, pushy bastards.
Pressure in a flow, then,
is an angry mob
with a mind of its own.

Bernoulli knew this but couldn't
come up with the equations.
You did, but they're useless,
not because they're for inviscids
but because they can't be solved,
an infinite stream of numbers

our closest approximation.

II. The Momentum Equation

$$\rho\frac{D\mu}{Dt} = -\frac{\partial p}{\partial x} \; ; \quad \rho\frac{Dv}{Dt} = -\frac{\partial p}{\partial y} \; ; \quad \rho\frac{D\omega}{Dt} = -\frac{\partial p}{\partial z}$$

F = ma applied to a moving fluid.

Throw Newton's Second Law in the river.
Better still, let's throw Newton, watch him
come up for air. He wasn't interested in flight,
only moving bodies, so we'll study his

as it's carried downstream, buoyed
by the current, the force you captured
in a formula and held in the hand
like water, only for a moment.

III. The Energy Equation

$$\rho\frac{D\left(e + {V^2}/{2}\right)}{Dt} = \rho q - \nabla \cdot (pV)$$

You wrote the perfect energy equation
by not writing one at all, saving your energy

for someone else, a hundred years later,
to do the work and give you credit.

Maybe you knew it's redundant anyway
for incompressible flow, that is, flight

before we learned how to make the air angry

by invading its personal space, pressing it

to go faster than it can. It wasn't the sun
that defeated Icarus but his arrogance,

flying higher than he should have and learning
the first law of thermodynamics the hard way.

D'ALEMBERT'S PARADOX, 1768

The Great Mathematician forgets about friction.

is no paradox
but Trickster's hand
meddling with the maths.

Right in theory, wrong in practice
gets you 50% Big Brains.
Better get up from the desk

and go for a swim,
if only to confirm
a fluid's resistance,

or take a few turns at bat,
striking out hard in three
whistling swings like the three papers

you published leading to the same
inexplicable conclusion: zero drag.
Today we can't resist

calling you Dummy
for neglecting friction,
dragging your pencil

across the page all day
only to end up in the evening
once again at 0.

THE NAVIER-STOKES EQUATIONS, 1822

In which friction is finally included.

When the 401 is fluid
you still get stuck in the slow lane
and flashed from behind by speedsters. Now imagine
pressure not from behind
but the side, the car chase in which
the bad guys force you off the road.

Imagine also
a solid passing through a fluid flow
as a roach motel through molecules. They get stuck
at the surface creating a slow lane
so slow it's the shoulder, and now

imagine a forest, farmland, or empty field
so beautiful you pull over and park,
abandoning your plans for the day,
your concerns, your car, maybe
even your life.

THE REYNOLDS NUMBER, 1883

$$\rho VD\ /\ \mu = 2,300$$

Turbulence is predicted.

When molecules refuse to march
in rank and file and break out
into field-show, forming umpteen
Olympic rings spinning out of control.

When the air, already anxious,
receives bad news: *must go faster!*
and suffers a breakdown,
becoming rapids, eddying over the wing.

When The System, suddenly destabilized
by the pace of progress,
erupts into anarchy, and angry
particles clash in the streets.

No one knows where or why,
but you knew when
things fall apart, the order
no longer holds: a product

greater than your name,
a number, a sign
to fasten our seat-belts and prepare
for all hell to break loose.

THE BOUNDARY LAYER EQUATIONS, 1904

A theory of surface friction.

Skin grows a skin
of air, but sticky air, a layer of anxiety
that holds you back, unawares
from pure speed, like the parking brake left on.

Then you will want to be the spawning salmon
surging through rapids with shape and skin
eluding their grasp, coining words
like "slipstream" and "streamline."

Leonardo will sketch your figure in his notebooks
next to a study of projectiles
and you will be, alas, forevermore the prototype
of bullet, bomb, missile, and airfoil—anything

that seeks deliverance or liberation, like caged birds
da Vinci would buy at the market
only to be released without spectacle,
ethic, symbolism, even aesthetic. Just released.

THE KUTTA-JOUKOWSKI THEOREM, 1906

$$L = \rho V \Gamma$$

Lift is mathematically proven.

I. *The Vortex Filament*

Clumsy air. Why can't it pass over a wing
without tripping, and falling, and somersaulting,
like a slapstick chorus line, into a wave
that breaks and breaks
and breaks into a roll?

Let's blame it on friction, someone's chewing gum
that catches the shoe and sends airflow
headlong into acrobatics.

II. *Circulatory Flow*

Air does its floor routine
tumbling over the wing to the edge
                         and over
causing a stir through the crowd which
sends out the wave, round and round the arena oh
a few thousand times. No one really
wants to do this but is compelled
to rise as the swell arrives, a force
that lifts us to our feet, spilling the refreshments,
our arms above our heads in an all hail
the hidden miracle of air!

III. *Flow Over an Airfoil*

Burn rubber over a speed bump.
Better yet, pop a wheelie
and attack the air with everything you've got,
which is only your wits
and will. Make it a tool, a servant, a slave
carrying you aloft like a Pharaoh.
Make it sweat. Be the boss
who says how high and no breaks,
the owner, hoarding all the profits.

You've earned it. All those years
working with water to pick its locks
and publish the secrets.
The time has come to figure this out, finally show
the proof. A number.
A name. Now
give the command: Lift.

THE LANCHESTER-PRANDTL LIFTING-LINE THEORY, 1918

$$\Gamma(y) = \frac{mc}{2}\left(U_\infty \alpha_0 - \frac{1}{4\pi} \int_{-\frac{b}{2}}^{\frac{b}{2}} \frac{d\Gamma}{dy_0} \frac{dy_0}{y - y_0} \right)$$

Finally, a theory of lift.

The wing is a leaky dam, spilling air
at the edges in swirls and eddies
that root and grow
into a tree. The tree

gets caught in a tornado
and becomes an electric beater, spinning its branches
and whipping the sea into waves
which foam and froth. The thicker the froth,

the harder the headway, slow-going
against nothing, churned until it curdles
into worry, a chronic anxiety
or sort of *Angst* which

gets the better of you,
the upper hand pressing down
for no good reason but
to force you back to earth.

Once you know this, you can fly.
Simply string the elements together
to construct a line of thought, a theory, a tool
to test the lift and drag upon a wing,
an airfoil, a dream, the heart.

THE COMPRESSIBILITY BURBLE, 1933

or, the ugliness at transonic flight.

Let's not argue whether transonic flow
has one s or two. It's nasty business,
a big unknown producing a belch
across the wing that turns heads
40,000 feet below. But this

is the least of our worries, a little after-effect
of a bit of undigested air. What's concerning
are all the graphs that point to stall, when air,
pumping weights, gets pooched,
and says Fuck it!, dropping everything.

This looks so bad it elicits euphemism,
a name that sounds like your wonky shock,
the burping warbler or baby toy—a rattle
that works only when thrown
at the speed of sound, which is the speed of air,

which is how far it's willing to carry us
before it balks, and bucks, and leaves us
midair with nothing
but a song and a prayer—that is,
a poem, a breath, the wind, or desire.

AUGURIES

SONG OF MY RESIDENT STARLING

after Don McKay

Spring arrived one morning in a torrent
from a starling's beak, bright yellow tweezers
that plucked me out of an armchair
and plonked me on the front lawn in my bathrobe.

Show-off. Perhaps he only wanted
to include me in his audience
as he ran through his repertoire,
or perhaps he was merely staking claim

to the *primo* spot behind my faciaboard.
Maybe I was drawn because
his song was similar to something
nesting in my throat. Stock-still,

mouth agape, I stood rooted—
sure that this must be a sign of more
than the mind of a bird, instinct,
or the start of a season.

For the finale, he took flight,
beating across the sky a drum roll for which
the cymbal crash, if it ever comes,
is the poem I want to write.

THE ALULA, OR BASTARD WING

Hallelujah's little half brother
midway along the wing
enables the bird, when things look bleak,
to give the thumbs up
so as not to stall, but let its dance partner,
the wind, pass gracefully beneath
with barely a twirl.

Which came first, the chicken
or the Handley-Page slot? When the airliner
descends in its final approach, gaze out
over the wing and watch
our poor imitation open along the leading edge.
About this time, you will feel the plane lurch
and slow, but not plummet.

Say a little prayer of thanks,
first to birds, then to those
who observed this tuft of feather
and wondered what it was for.
Or praise the Lord (under your breath).
As a sign of reverence, press your hand
against the pane and leave
an imprint of your own infant wing.

WHITE STORK

In the distance, you are the double frown
of birds in children's drawings—all wings
trying to be a conductor's arms
performing the adagio of flight. You sad
silly bird. You like living on the edge,
nesting on power lines that can cripple a wing with one
                              false
step, a high-wire act for the tourists.
Better to go back to chimneys
where you are only victim of folklore
and village gossip, blamed
for each unwanted pregnancy.

Perched motionless
on your oversized woven coaster, you are
a bent coat-hanger, an antenna, a weathervane
with attitude, pointing down.
Too bad you have to land at all
to feed and nest. Soaring on thermals, you seem
a mere million years away
from a life of pure flight
when all your comic gestures, melancholy, daring,
    and genius
will be churned into myth.

CROW

after Ted Hughes

Crow is a garbage bag flapping in the wind.
Crow is a quarter note perched on the wire.
Crow is an oily rag flung onto the fir.
Crow is an ink splotch spoiling the virgin page.

Crow is a botch, work spelt backwards
wrong. Crow drives the nail in crooked
and sets the plumb-bob askew. Crow
is the accident waiting to happen:
fingertips in the Skilsaw, splinter in the eye.
Crow eats roadkill for breakfast.

Crow is smart. Crow outwits the seagull
for french fries. Crow uses tools,
can imitate English better than the parrot,
but keeps it a secret.
Crow uses cars to crack nuts, can count and knows
the number of hunters left in the blind.

Crow is a guide with attitude, a messenger
with a sick sense of humour. Crow says
"Give up" to piss you off and try harder.
Crow says "Watch me—" strikes a pose,
and shits. Crow says "Tomorrow" in a dying language
to tease us on toward night
as black as Crow.

ODE TO A DYING PIGEON

I'm rushing to the bus when you flare up from the corner of consciousness, taking my breath like a gust of wind in the face, perhaps the last eddy of air you'll make. Your two-toned grey plumage seems the product of a million-odd years of hard evolution toward city life. Nestled in the corner of a storefront step, you look just like concrete or garbage, your two principal elements. Only the subtle turquoise encircling your neck gives you away, a colour found only in cosmetics and certain seashells.

You are the tough inner-city homeless of birds, surviving the harshest winters with barely a handout from a few sympathetic tourists and eccentrics. Maybe because you are so hardy we think you need nothing at all but a place to perch and shit. Your song is a coo with indigestion, barely a guttural gurgle, you wouldn't want to disturb anyone or draw attention to yourself. In fact, you might go an entire life without notice, blending in perfectly to the drab backdrop of urban existence. But here you are, squatting in your feces and a rotting apple core. You open your eyes and take me in, squint, shake your head, and puff yourself larger. Who are you trying to kid? We both know the end is near.

And what an ignominious place it is to die: a crowded sidewalk amid morning rush hour. The heels of people waiting for the bus are inches from your face and there's nothing you can do about it. Where is all your agility now, that capacity to elude cars at the last possible moment in three flaps or less? You couldn't even avoid my foot if I took one small step, slowly bringing it down, which perhaps I would if I had half your grit.

BATS

They come from the deepest, darkest places in nature,
from caves, forest, and night. No wonder
they are archetypal, appearing cloaked and necromantic
in our folklore and nightmares. Their erratic flight
resembles the rhythm of our terrified hearts,
scribing an EKG across the blue-black page.
Even in sleep, still and silent as stalactites,
they have the uncanny capacity to unnerve.

Half rodent, half bird, they bridge the lower and upper register
of evolution with fur, sharp teeth, echolocation, and flight.
And because we think they are blind, they embody
perhaps our greatest fear—a life without light.
Even their anorexic wings remind us of
the worst part of ourselves, and for this
we lift them into myth, creatures of imagination,
buying and selling their framed corpses on eBay.

FLY DYING ON THE BEDROOM FLOOR

You who can cartwheel onto the ceiling. You who can deke from standstill the swatting hand or newspaper. You who can turn verb into noun through feats of flying cannot, for the life of you, fly now.

I hear your distress, a buzz-roll on the hardwood, and recognize in its rhythm of fits and pauses a plea for three-dimensional space. When it weakens, it becomes the snore of my sleeping, shadow self, the one who wants to fly, to *be* fly, to be dark, diseased, dangerous. Is this your song, the punk version of Flight of the Bumblebee? Unplugged, but amplified by the dark, it could be the perfect accompaniment to a panic attack, night terror, or the dream in which I can't remember my name.

I imagine you, probably caught under the curtains, spinning on your back like a manic break-dancer. Or perhaps you are carving geometric shapes, figure skater on amphetamines, wearing a costume woven entirely from hair. This must be the long program, the one in which you eventually die of exhaustion at the end of a climactic, blinding spin, striking a pose, legs extended in the air, on the final note for eternity.

If my dog were here, he would reincarnate you as worm in his stool. You would become intimate with his entrails. He would lift you clean from my bedroom floor and deposit you at the park. But he has preceded you to that place you are going, and now that you have reminded me of this sadness, *musca domesticas,* I want you out of my house. I want sleep to knit up the sleeve of care you have unraveled with your spinning. I will put an end to this, even if I must heave myself from bed and hunt, bare-assed on all fours, for what's left of you.

SNOWBIRDS

A flock of retirees has stolen your name.
Better that than budget cuts and public apathy,
two pillars of Canadian culture. Perhaps you should
play the patriotism hand a little firmer, fly
a formation in the shape of maple leaf, pine tree,
ear of wheat, or hockey stick with solo pilot
as puck, although you have one now named Goose,
another in the arrowhead of their migration before you
explode into fireworks, draw a trellis, scratch a heart
into the sky or unfold a fan so gracefully we forget
this is military. Once you dropped bombs. Today,
you inspire children to play smart, play safe,
shaking hands in crimson flight suits as you work the
    crowd,
"Warriors of the Air" stitched in Iroquois over your hearts.

BOMBS AWAY

The first is for Franz,
	may he rest in peace, a little payback
	for Princip's bullets, with interest.

We know you didn't do it and
	this is not Sarajevo, but consider it
	collateral damage or strategic targeting.

Fallout. The second is for your snooty attitude
	and nasal whining, looking down your noses
	on everyone as if you were *übermenschen*.

The third is a little *strafen* —punishment.
Your offence? Being French
	and an ally of those who steal from our language.

The fourth is for the boys dug in
	outside your walls. I promised I'd send one
	special delivery, signed "Open Sesame."

The fourth is for the future, the shape of things to come:
the Zeppelins, the Gothas, the Blitz,
	carpet bombing, cluster bombs, incendiary bombs,

the firestorms of Dresden that made cement melt
	and windows drip. For Shock and Awe,
	smart bombs, the cruise and The Unforgettable Fire.

And this one, the last? This
	is for another death: a symbol
	of human marvel, the miracle

of flight, of God knows—
everything
other than this.

SOME USES FOR A KITE

To discover electricity, and demonstrate its power
by killing those who reproduce the experiment
if not knocking them on their butts.

To entertain the Chinese Emperor
with the 150-foot failures of early man-lifting models
strapped to the backs of political prisoners—

except for one, whose was an owl with wingspan
wide enough to carry him safely
into history as the world's first successful flight.

To calculate the distance to the fortress walls and know
how long the tunnel must be. To observe enemy lines and,
why not?, drop some bombs on them too.

To serve as target practice for warship gunners
and deliver papers from ship to plane, snagged
like a mosquito in a swallow's beak. And when

at last, men are not fighting men,
to fight each other, slashed to ground
by lines loaded with sand, glass, blades.

To receive the first transatlantic telegram.
To span a gorge (as Leonardo said) and start Niagara
    Bridge,
then a while later, do it again

for the cable car. To take the temperature of the sky,
the first photograph of the earth from God's perspective,
that is, the birds'. To thieve from rooftops,

drop billets-doux to a secluded lover, be found when lost
at sea, a floatation device, the horse of a horseless
carriage, a dog-team to the North Pole and pull

Captain Cody, King of the Cowboys, across The Channel.
To lift a man from the ship's deck, invoking spirits
for safe and prosperous passage. To ward off evil, ensure

a good harvest and give thanks for one, congratulate
new parents, celebrate The Taliban
pulling out of Kabul and, above all,

remind us how to play, tugging
our clenched fists into the air, champions
of nothing at all.

BOOMERANG

Some elusive combination
of force, rotation, angle, and wind
will get this thing to return,
an equation whose product is 0.
But now the result is embarrassment,
everyone at the park, I'm sure, watching
the cycles of my failure.
They know what it's supposed to do.
I send it out again—cart-wheeling along the horizon,
a propeller without a plane, the bodiless wing
of some bird of prey
I'm trying to train.

*

What goes around comes around,
but this, early aboriginal weapon,
returns to us as play, a toy
we use to kill time.
Only a game could have
the point of origin its goal
and make each of us the target,
its flight path an odyssey,
the journey in which we
overcome all obstacles
and return home, at last,
hero of the park.

FRISBEE

The ancient Greeks had the right idea
but the wrong technique. Why the whirling dervish
when a flick of the wrist will do?
That's all it takes when your discus
is a wing with a 360° airfoil.

The first to figure this out
were some truckers whose boredom at the docks
was the mother of their invention, a pie plate turned
into a toy that turned
into The Flying Saucer that turned
into The Pluto Platter that turned
into The Frisbee, named after the baker
whose pie plates became
toys for bored truckers.

Is it more fun to throw or catch?
Maybe it's the moment in between, when the wind,
the invisible third, plays as well, and we
become audience, watch how it holds
its breath—the whole note rest—or sends the Frisbee up
and down the scales in a kind of jazz
for the deaf. When it hovers above,
floats down, and lights upon your finger,
you think of the hummingbird you're trying to tame,
and the trick with a spinning basketball
you've always wanted to do.

But the most fun comes
oddly from the errant throw, the one
that makes you run, and leap—

and for a moment you are airborne too,
stretching to meet the Frisbee,

when it comes to you, at the apex of your own arc,
that the toy is really air, a playspace
equal only to water, that lifts and carries us
elsewhere.

AUGURIES

All winter they were missing, the cacophony in the
    climbing ivy
suddenly absent like the foil plates full of seeds
I placed beneath the feeders to attract them
that blew away. I thought of La Niña, Mother Nature's
    cold shoulder,
and a layman's description of Arctic air
sucked down into a vacuum, of carrier pigeons
that disappeared one race, discovered days later
in twos and threes on doorsteps of another continent,
and our birdless Christmas in the country, void of the
    usual
goldfinches, cowbirds, grosbeaks, and grackles.

That morning I spotted a small flock of black specks
huddled on a rooftop in blowing chimney-smoke,
and later on the mountain the sound of a single
but unmistakable woodpecker, stray signs
in the sentence trying to shape itself all day,
which now is uttered in a gasp as I'm arrested,
halfway to the curb with the garbage,
by the cedar full of squabbling sparrows.

1000' IN AN ULTRALIGHT

This must be what Orville felt
in that toothpick and fabric contraption
once he got the damn thing
up. This is no airliner, no
flying bus, plane-
cum-living room, this
is flying by the seat of your pants, the only thing
separating my butt from the ground below
save a plastic seat and 1000 feet
of slow, spectacular death.

I look down: it's like being at the top of the CN Tower,
minus the tower. What the hell
am I doing here? Why
have I trusted my life to this stranger, this
kite with an engine, and the will of air?

When we hit turbulence, my faith in Christ
Almighty get me down does
this guy have a licence I
know now what the Monarch
goes through, stomach
in mouth—Oh
God I promise never
to underrate gravity
again.

KITE-FLYING

A long time ago my son and I
took our kites to the park and
let them out. Hand over hand,
they backed away into blue sky.

It was a warm, summer day
and my work, his school had
also receded, so it was just us
and our kites, the park, the wind, and sky.

When the spools were empty we
lay on our backs in the grass, the blades
tickling our bare legs and watched
the kites sway and bob above.

We lay there for so long that we
became hungry, but since it had
taken so long to set the kites high
above the trees where the wind

is sure and steady, we pushed one end
of each spool into the earth, angled
like a nail driven into a wall to hold a picture,
or the barb of fish-hook set fast in flesh.

Which was stronger, the wind
or the earth? We let go and watched
carefully should the spools pull free,
tumbling across the fields

as the lines drooped slack, the kites
rocked and fluttered, dipped and

dropped toward the distant highway
and lake beyond. But they held—

so we walked the few blocks
back to the house, and when we arrived,
before making the sandwiches, we climbed
the stairs to the second floor

where we had a good view
across rooftops to our kites, still there
in the distance, the lines now invisible,
just two specks side-by-side, hovering

alone over the neighbourhood.

TWO TURTLEDOVES

Everyone thought I was crazy
to give a pregnant woman birds, warned
of diseases released from feces

that could turn a fetus deaf.
And wasn't the paper
just another diaper to change?

It was our first Christmas
and the promise of new life bound
us together in a Côte-des-Neiges apartment.

Their home I made on the sly,
a simple design of wood dowelling
drilled into plywood and painted red.

I was thinking of the carol, of course,
but more the cooing of your childhood mornings
from pigeons nesting above the bedroom window,

and the dream in which the sky is filled with birds
feeding from your hand
you had upon hearing you were pregnant.

I won't say I made a mistake, not even
in hindsight. The life we made
outgrew its home, took flight

one sunny afternoon, and could not
be coaxed back. The other
was snatched off her perch by the dog

and brought to me, a death
carried gently and placed
at my feet as an unexpected gift.

MATING FUGUE

Two mayflies clung to my front door for days. Each time
I left the house, I was careful not to slam the door. Finally
I thought they might be dead so I reached out with a
single finger like an antenna and stroked one. It slowly
opened and closed its wings, as if taking a breath, exposing
the delicate webbing. Nothing could be more delicate,
I thought. The next day I found, as if in reply, that they
had gone, leaving behind their shed, ghost-like selves.

❧

Two wild doves nested in my bathroom window, kept
ajar for weeks. Each morning I would see her sitting on
the eggs, but even before that it was often her mournful
song that lifted me toward waking. One day I returned
home and found the yard littered with feathers and the
male badly mauled. I filled a pot with water and held him
under until the bubbles stopped, thinking of their name in
French, *tourterelle triste*. I wondered if she would continue
to nest. The next day I found her dead on the street, swept
her carcass into the ditch.

❧

Two sparrows nested in my birdhouse for years. Each
spring I'd see them mating, nuptial kisses at the end of
a flutter of wings. When she went away, he'd sit on a
branch outside the home and call, a relentless chirp like a
squeaky wheel spinning for hours. Once while fixing the
porch I grabbed a 2 x 4 from the stack behind the shed
and found, while hammering it into place, downy feathers
and fledgling crap splattered on it, a sign saying From Our
House to Yours.

❧

She said it was a cockroach but I didn't agree. Then we saw it had wings. I would have captured it in a glass and carried it outside, but before I could stop her she stepped on it, as if extinguishing a cigarette. The carapace crunched under her toe and I knew we would never be lovers.

LANDING

I.

Years of flying to and from each other—
we finally fly together. Nothing is normal.

The sad good-bye at Departures
is for the friend who drops us off.
I do not watch you disappear through sliding doors
nor turn back for a final glance, but walk with you
into the florescent maze of airport.

We know the procedure, but this time
your presence is a new element
disturbing the order. At Security
I forget to remove my computer,
I forget to remove my watch,
I forget to replace my computer
and have to be paged back to retrieve it.

Nothing is normal. During flight
I do not write in my journal.
I do not plug in to TV. The unoccupied seat
is on the aisle and when I gaze out the window
there is someone with whom to share
geometric landforms below, clouds
the colour of thistle and hydrangeas.

The plane banks into its final approach
and now the landmarks are familiar,
the mountain where you photographed
chickadees eating from my hand,

the Oratoire, the college—my office,
fifth window from the right, where you waited
while I taught a class that first visit, years ago,
when this moment was just a vision:
a plane touching down, two people walking off.

II.

I wake up trembling from another dream
of flying. It is so simple I wonder why

it took me so long to see
that flight is not up but down, falling

into the body, the heart
not an engine at all but a bird

cupped in two hands. I'm trembling
because at last I see

that I am the bird
embraced by something benevolent and terrifying

and flight is this song, my entire being
breathed into the wind.

NOTES

"$L = k \times S \times V^2 \times C_L$"

$L = k \times S \times V^2 \times C_L$ is known as the Lift Equation. Wilbur Wright came across this equation amongst the papers procured by request from the Smithsonian Institution and used it to calculate the wingspan of his first glider in 1900. The components are as follows:

L = Lift in pounds

k = Coefficient of air pressure

S = Total area of lifting surface

V^2 = Velocity (headwind plus airspeed) squared

C_L = Coefficient of lift

"Paris, le 22 octobre 1880"

Alphonse Pénaud, crippled by a degenerative hip disease, was France's most talented and promising aeronautical inventor of the late 19th Century. After building and demonstrating the world's first powered model airplane at the age of 21, he designed a full-size airplane that had many features not common until the mid-20th Century. Unable to secure funding to build it, he turned to early airship inventor Henri Giffard as a last hope. When Giffard refused to help, Pénaud built a small coffin in which he placed his drawings, delivered it to Giffard's house, then returned home and took his life at the age of 30.

"The Spirit of Saint Louis"

Charles Lindbergh claimed that during his trans-Atlantic flight he had an out-of-body experience in which he had the sensation that he "existed independently of time and matter" and that he was visited by spirits that consoled and encouraged him.

"Dear George: the Lost Letter"
Amelia Earhart was selected to be the first woman to fly the Atlantic (as a passenger) by her future husband, the publicist George Putnam of Putnam Publishing. She was chosen primarily based on her physical resemblance to Charles Lindbergh, whose nickname was Lucky Lindy. Consequently, Earhart was nicknamed by the press Lady Lindy.

"White Stork" is dedicated to Don McKay.

"Crow"
In Ancient Rome, the crow's croak was said to sound like the Latin *cras* ("tomorrow"), linking it with hope.

"Bombs Away"
On August 30, 1914, not six years after Orville Wright unveiled the first military airplane, a German pilot dropped several bombs and a derisive note on Paris, executing the first aerial bombing of a capital city.

"Kite-Flying" is dedicated to Gabriel.

"Landing" is dedicated to Marilyn.

Acknowledgments

This book builds upon the hard work and passion of many others who have written about the history of flight and aerodynamics. In particular, I am indebted to Richard P. Hallion's *Taking Flight: Inventing the Aerial Age from Antiquity Through the First World War* (Oxford UP), John D. Anderson, Jr.'s *A History of Aerodynamics* (Cambridge UP), and Tom Crouch's *The Bishop's Boys: A Life of Wilbur and Orville Wright* (Norton).

Some of these poems have appeared in *The Fiddlehead, The Prairie Journal, Prairie Fire, The Antigonish Review, Prism International,* and *Exile.* I am grateful to the editors of these journals.

Thanks also to The Canada Council for the Arts for a grant which enabled me to finish the manuscript.

These poems have been shaped by the sensitive reading of many individuals. Thanks to early readers Jane Barclay, Pierre Paré, and Lori Weber, and to subsequent readers, Katia Grubisic, Harold Hoefle, Gary Geddes, and Brian Bartlett.

Finally, a special thanks to my wife, Marilyn Gillespie, for her constant support and encouragement.

Kevin Bushell's poems have appeared in *The Fiddlehead, The Antigonish Review, Prairie Fire,* and *Exile,* among other journals. His poem "The Life of Alberto Santos-Dumont: A Tragedy in Two Acts" was published in *The Best Canadian Poetry in English 2011,* edited by Priscila Uppal. He teaches at Vanier College in Montreal and lives in Pointe-Claire, Quebec.